MW01226999

# *Cursive Handwriting for Girls*

## CHILDREN'S READING & WRITING EDUCATION BOOKS

**PROFESSOR GUSTO**
EDUCATIONAL & INFORMATIVE BOOKS FOR CHILDREN
(PRE-K / K-12)

Trace the cursive
letters and words.
Rewrite the letters and
words in the space provided.

*Aa Aa Aa Aa Aa*

*Aa*

*A*

*a*

*A is for Apple*

*Bb Bb Bb Bb*

*Bb*

*B*

*b*

*B is for Banana*

Cc Cc Cc Cc Cc

Cc

C

c

C is for Coffee

Dd Dd Dd Dd

Dd

D

d

D is for Donut

Ee Ee Ee Ee Ee

Ee

E

e

E is for Egg

Ff Ff Ff Ff Ff

Ff

F

f

F is for Flower

Gg Gg Gg Gg

Gg

G

g

G is for Grapes

*Hh Hh Hh Hh*

*Hh*

*H*

*h*

*H is for Honey*

Ii Ii Ii Ii Ii Ii

Ii

I

i

I is for Ice Cream

Jj Jj Jj Jj Jj Jj

Jj

J

j

J is for Juice

Kk Kk Kk Kk Kk

Kk

K

k

K is for Kangaroo

Ll Ll Ll Ll Ll

Ll

L

l

L is for Leaf

*Mm Mm Mm*

*Mm*

*M*

*m*

*M is for Mouse*

Nn Nn Nn Nn

Nn

N

n

N is for Nest

*Oo Oo Oo Oo Oo*

*Oo*

*O*

*o*

*O is for Omelette*

*P p*   *P p*   *P p*   *P p*   *P p*

*P p*

*P*

*P*

*P is for Peacock*

*Qq* *Qq* *Qq* *Qq* *Qq*

*Qq*

*Q*

*q*

*Q is for Queen*

*Rr* *Rr* *Rr* *Rr* *Rr*

*Rr*

*R*

*r*

*R is for Rainbow*

Ss   Ss   Ss   Ss   Ss

Ss

S

s

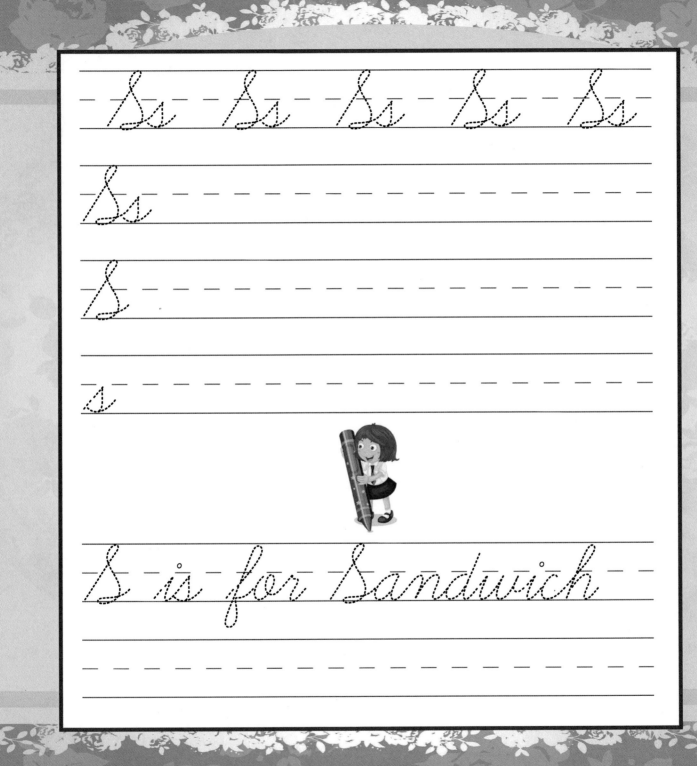

S is for Sandwich

Tt  Tt  Tt  Tt  Tt  Tt

Tt

T

t

T is for Teapot

*Uu Uu Uu Uu*

*Uu*

*U*

*u*

*U is for Umbrella*

*Vv Vv Vv Vv*

*Vv*

*V*

*v*

*V is for Vase*

*Ww Ww Ww*

*Ww*

*W*

*w*

*W is for Watermelon*

*Xx Xx Xx Xx*

*Xx*

*X*

*x*

*X is for Xylophone*

*Yy Yy Yy Yy Yy*

*Yy*

*Y*

*y*

*Y is for Yoyo*

$\mathscr{Z}z$    $\mathscr{Z}z$    $\mathscr{Z}z$    $\mathscr{Z}z$    $\mathscr{Z}z$

$\mathscr{Z}z$

$\mathscr{Z}$

$z$

$\mathscr{Z}$ is for $\mathscr{Z}$ipper

Trace the cursive
sentences and rewrite them
in the space provided.

*Hannah is eating.*

*Grace is playing.*

*Linda is working.*

*This is a book.*

*I am a girl.*

*I'm good at tennis.*

*The door is opened.*

*I brush my teeth.*

*I comb my hair.*